3
MEDITATIONS
FOR
TEACHERS

By Greg Henry Quinn

SCHOLASTIC INC.
New York Toronto London Auckland Sydney

No part of this publication may be reproduced in whole or in part, or stored in a retrieval system, or transmitted in any form or by any means, electronic, mechanical, photocopying, recording, or otherwise, without written permission of the publisher. For information regarding permission, write to Scholastic Inc., 555 Broadway, New York, NY 10012.

ISBN 0-590-25508-8

Copyright © 1995 by Gregory H. Quinn.
All rights reserved. Published by Scholastic Inc.

12 11 10 9 8 7   9/9 0/0
                                                      01

Printed in the U.S.A.
First Scholastic printing, September 1995

*To the teachers
who taught me to love words,
that I may use them
to touch another.*

• INTRODUCTION •

*"Every teacher should realize
the dignity of his calling."*
— John Dewey

Teaching is the greatest of all professions. Only by studying the sciences, developing sensitivity for the arts, and learning the histories can a people progress beyond themselves.

The awesome responsibility of passing on this knowledge to each new generation in a form that may be absorbed, remembered, and eventually improved upon belongs mostly to the teachers. Since the beginning of humankind, societies have entrusted the education of their children to those gifted few who possess not only the knowledge but the desire and wisdom necessary for this most sacred of professions.

Today, teachers are under tremendous pressure to perform within ever more difficult constraints. Classes are larger, parental participation is not always evident, and students generally have more complex problems and less respect for authority than before. Personal strength and peace in this environment are prerequisites for controlling one's life and maintaining control with those to be taught. It is my hope that these meditations may serve as buoys, anchors, and lighthouses for teachers on their personal voyages through life.

The thoughts herein are a collection of original offerings blended with those of actual teachers and scholars of renown. As you wander through the meditations and observations, you will note that I often refer to teachers as masters, and so they are.

In many of the Eastern cultures, the highest member of society is the master. Merchants, artisans, craftspeople, medical practitioners, and others were all once disciples of the masters. It is right, therefore, that teachers occupy this place, for only through education can civilization thrive.

G.H.Q.

January

A Teacher's Motto

"Each and every day . . .
Each and every child.
I have the power, the passion, the skill, and the
  knowledge
to make a difference.
Each and every day . . .
Each and every child."

— Sandra McBrayer,
1994 United States Teacher of the Year

Get the thing done!

We are each in possession of a finite amount of energy at any given moment. To accomplish a task, it is not so much the quantity of energy but how it is used. The greatest waste of energy is spent fleeing from the task.

To give is golden.

Develop the habit of giving of yourself with no need of reward, and your rewards will be more than you ever needed.

*Children are the future as inevitably as
the future is change.*

The difference between being taught to
conform to the confines of society and
being taught to change society for the
better within its confines is values.

*Few have more opportunities to be heroes
than do teachers.*

Heroes are those who put themselves on
the line to accomplish difficult, and sometimes impossible, tasks. While it's not expected that teachers shed blood, they are
known to contribute more than their
share of sweat and tears.

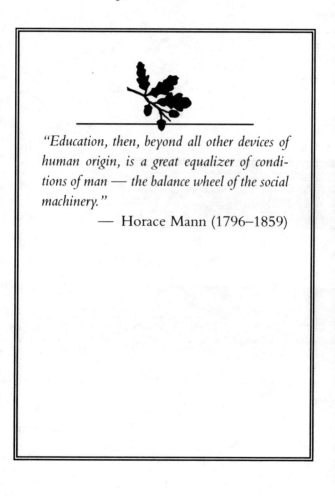

"Education, then, beyond all other devices of human origin, is a great equalizer of conditions of man — the balance wheel of the social machinery."

— Horace Mann (1796–1859)

Never threaten; promise.

Authority is only an illusion when it lacks conviction of intent.

Be one with your students only in truth.

A community will pay homage to a leader who empathizes with their lives. But beware — this must be sincere or not at all. The slightest falsity will be a brand forever.

The urge to quit is the signal that an opportunity to excel is at hand.

Obstacles present choices. They can mark the end of the road or the beginning of a new period of growth. Those who have few obstacles are the least fortunate. Growth can only take place while transcending obstacles.

The lesson of how to use knowledge is as important as the knowledge itself.

When children have a good foundation of values, they have a solid basis for the proper use of knowledge.

Anger is the logical expression of frustration.

When a teacher expresses anger, the lesson is anger. When a teacher expresses wisdom, the lesson is respect. Anticipating problems allows one to prepare solutions in advance. It is through this preparedness that the master remains in control, commands respect, and avoids frustration and anger. Make a list of all the problems you can imagine and create solutions. This list will grow with time and wisdom.

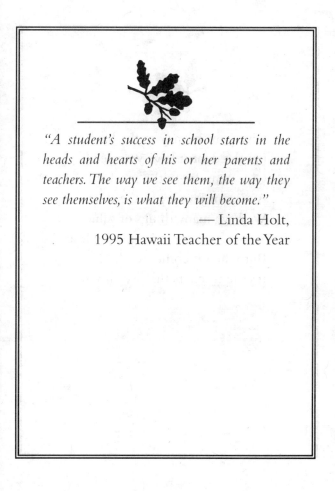

"*A student's success in school starts in the heads and hearts of his or her parents and teachers. The way we see them, the way they see themselves, is what they will become.*"

— Linda Holt,
1995 Hawaii Teacher of the Year

Give your money to the banker.
Let the dentist have your teeth.
Give your car to the mechanic,
And your jewelry to the thief.
We have many things of value,
Some we keep and some we lose.
But when it comes to children
It's the teachers that we choose.

For children to experience growth, they must experience consequences.

It is within the purview of all teachers to establish a system of rules and consequences that will encourage thoughtful decision-making.

"My ideas on teaching and learning focus on small 'd' democratic values, by which I mean a respect for diversity, a respect for the potential of each individual person, a respect for opposing points of view, and a respect for considerable intellectual vigor. My concern is with how students become critical thinkers and problem solvers, which is what a democratic society needs."

— Deborah Willen Meier

Life is more than a song; it is a concert!

Play all the sharps and flats of your life with the strength, beauty, and confidence of the masters, and it will be a masterpiece.

As you assess your life, assess yourself.

————————————

The view of our circumstances, our performance, our direction, and our accomplishments is determined by our viewpoint. For the most part, we are the products of ourselves.

Don't just teach; be.

When parents raise a child, that child imitates and adopts some of the parents' ways. So, too, when a teacher teaches a student, what is learned is always greater than what was in the book.

The best example is experience.

To know the best way to correct a student, examine yourself. We have all made similar mistakes in our lives. What approach would you have responded to?

"Let early education be a sort of amusement; you will then be better able to find out the natural bent."

— Plato, *The Republic*

Seek not quick rewards, but quick smiles.

A full and happy life is one in which instant gratification is never a goal, but the ability to enjoy a spontaneous burst of mirth is always at hand. Approach each day with humor.

You can't re-create the past, but you can incorporate it into the future.

We all have a time in our life that we would like to go back to — "the way we were." This longing for the past retards our progress into the inevitable future. Mold the uncertain future with the good points of the past, and you will be using your experience to live as you like.

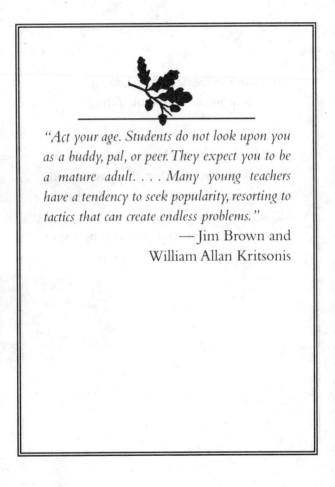

"*Act your age. Students do not look upon you as a buddy, pal, or peer. They expect you to be a mature adult. . . . Many young teachers have a tendency to seek popularity, resorting to tactics that can create endless problems.*"

— Jim Brown and
William Allan Kritsonis

Every single life has a purpose.

Few experiences are more profound and more confusing to a child than death. The weight of the child's emotions often falls heavily on the teacher. To speak of death has far less meaning than to speak of the significance and value of life. Death is merely the final of many milestones in a physical life.

Children expect to be told where they fit in.

If a child perceives that his goal is to make enough money to buy a nice car, then that is where he sets his sights. If he perceives that his goal is to design that car . . .

What you have may be a sign of what you are lacking.

The most well-off have as much to learn from the underprivileged as the opposite. When the wealthy endeavor to understand the poor, they inspire rather than alienate.

Love is the cause and result of energy.

Love of oneself, love of another, love of work, and love of life are the driving forces for those at peace. Learn to feel love and you will know how to live life.

Christa McAuliffe (1949–1986)

It is fitting that the first private citizen chosen to go up into space was a teacher. It is prophetic that the ultimate sacrifice was paid by that teacher while representing the value of the teachers of the world.

Be at peace with yourself before endeavoring to bring peace to others.

You will be better equipped to help a drowning person if you have first learned to swim. If you are charitable at the cost of all your assets, you can only be charitable once and then become a burden on others.

Discipline is the rudimentary thread of the learning cloak.

There are many successful styles and methods of teaching. Each incorporates discipline, be it self-discipline, or administered, or a little of both.

It is an amusement to betray one's superior.
It is anathema to betray one's peers.

The inimitable force of peer pressure is always present. When manipulated wisely, it will strengthen the community and lessen the struggles.

February

Know thy convictions!

If a teacher is guided by a true passion to teach and bans the darkness with the light of knowledge, then nothing can extinguish that flame, nothing.

The first rule in a productive community is peace.

To be a teacher is to wear many hats. Be a peacemaker, and the crown of a leader will fit comfortably.

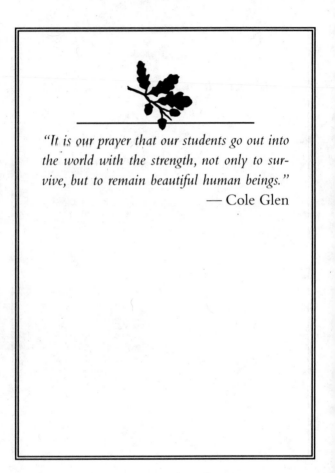

"*It is our prayer that our students go out into the world with the strength, not only to survive, but to remain beautiful human beings.*"
— Cole Glen

*Before fear is taught, a child is unaware
of limitations.*

It is the nature of children to reach for
that which is beyond their grasp. Expect
more of your students and they will aspire to greater heights.

The mind is the great equalizer.

Children are acutely aware of their short-comings in relation to their peers. Not everyone has the innate athletic ability to overcome physical limitations of size and strength, but since we all use so little of our mental potential anyway, there is always room for dramatic mind growth. When students learn this, it will be difficult to hold them back.

Work leads to greater success than nonwork. Hard work leads to greatness.

The great lesson in work ethic is to push beyond the point of first fatigue.

Focus on solutions, not problems.

With the knowledge that life is inherently problematic, even specific unexpected problems become expected in general. Train your mind to reactively seek solutions rather than just react to problems.

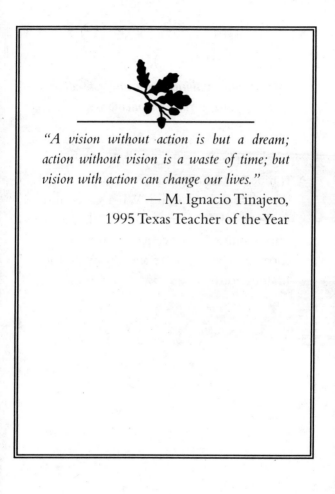

"A vision without action is but a dream; action without vision is a waste of time; but vision with action can change our lives."

— M. Ignacio Tinajero,
1995 Texas Teacher of the Year

Repetition combined with understanding creates permanent memories.

When a lesson is introduced, it may be absorbed by the conscious mind. When it is repeated many times, it is absorbed by the unconscious mind. When it is also understood, it opens and frees the conscious mind to concentrate on new information and incorporate it with the unconscious.

The guiding hand that is firm is the hand that is reached for.

Children seek consistency and stability in their lives. Consistent discipline will be respected more than consistent acquiescence.

Sacrifice is the price of gain.

The most important lessons in life are the most painful. Lessons that come without risks are of little consequence for real growth.

No matter how small, acknowledge the achievement.

A sense of accomplishment creates the velocity to excel past complacency.

Thoughts must be transmitted and received for teaching to take place.

To be effective, communication must be carried out in a common language spoken at a common level. If students don't listen, it is an attention problem; if they don't hear, it is a communication problem.

Never question whether to give love.

Each act of love is like a crumb of bread for the birds of winter. The offering is cheap to give and invaluable to receive.

Life is meant to be lived.

———————————

Those who deal with pain the best are those that have accepted pain as a natural part of life. These are the ones who enjoy pleasure the most.

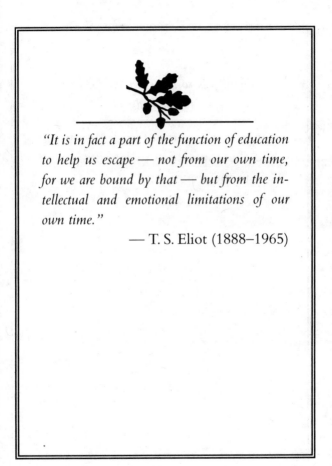

"*It is in fact a part of the function of education to help us escape — not from our own time, for we are bound by that — but from the intellectual and emotional limitations of our own time.*"

— T. S. Eliot (1888–1965)

*Dignity is to the spirit as food is
to the body.*

Dignity is the source of pride that gives a child the confidence to take his or her place in the community.

Spend more time examining yourself and less time seeking approval of your actions.

Frequent self-examination breeds familiarity with your daily thoughts and actions. While every action you take will not result in success, with each you gain the confidence of independent action, which better prepares you for future endeavors.

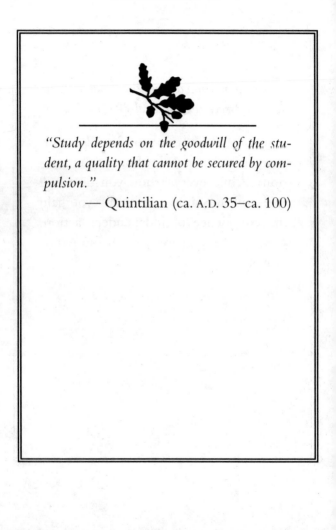

"*Study depends on the goodwill of the student, a quality that cannot be secured by compulsion.*"

— Quintilian (ca. A.D. 35–ca. 100)

Manage your time and you will be managing your life.

Management is the secret to productivity. Rarely is there too little time, but often there is time used unwisely.

Place no one above the objective.

It is not required that you love everyone equally, but if you love what you do, your dedication will ensure that all get your best effort.

Be thankful for the bad times, for they herald the onset of the good.

All things change always. The question is not if the storm will end but when. Think of the storm as the harbinger of the calm, and life will be more predictable than frustrating.

A quiet friend may sometimes be a desirable friend.

When advice is not asked for, it's usually not well received. Often, people know what they must do to solve a problem but look for less painful solutions. Your silent support will allow them to hear their own hearts.

Enthusiasm can be generated by will and perpetuated by itself.

Enthusiasm is the invisible source of energy that children find so attractive and contagious. You light the match, and they will carry the torch.

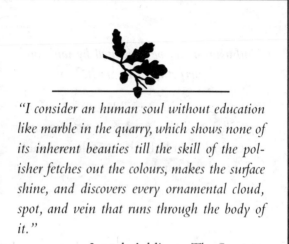

"I consider an human soul without education like marble in the quarry, which shows none of its inherent beauties till the skill of the polisher fetches out the colours, makes the surface shine, and discovers every ornamental cloud, spot, and vein that runs through the body of it."

— Joseph Addison, *The Spectator*

To know real love is to know loss.

The awareness of two-dimensional love exists in us all. Many times we must lose that which we love to truly perceive depth. If you always avoid situations in which you might lose, you will rarely win and never love.

Strength is built when strength is tested.

With responsibility comes greater burden. With the acceptance of this increased load come the feelings of newfound strength, then independence, then self-worth.

"*Avoid negative responses. Touch them. Let them know you care. Always use positive reinforcement.*"

— Lillie Rayborn

March

Outside the classroom the student must live in the world; inside the classroom the student can own the world.

Nowhere else has more to offer than school: everything that has existed in the past, everything that is available in the present, and the limitless possibilities of the future. One only needs to convince the student of the value of these riches.

Laziness makes you lazy; involvement makes you ambitious.

Students who have the most trouble managing their time usually don't have enough to do.

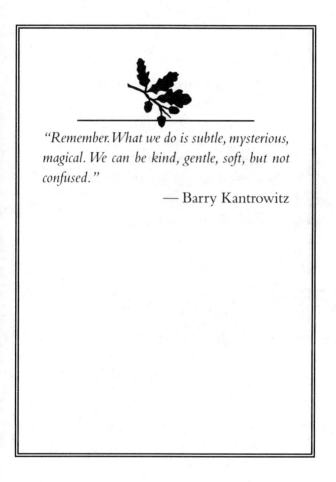

"Remember. What we do is subtle, mysterious, magical. We can be kind, gentle, soft, but not confused."

— Barry Kantrowitz

Savor your passion, then share it.

Those teachers who have and share a true passion for the subject matter become the inspirations for tomorrow's great.

It is much easier to take a step than to climb a mountain — or is it?

We all have the ability to advance one step, but for most of us ascending a mountain seems beyond our capabilities. Every mountain crested began with one step and ended with one step.

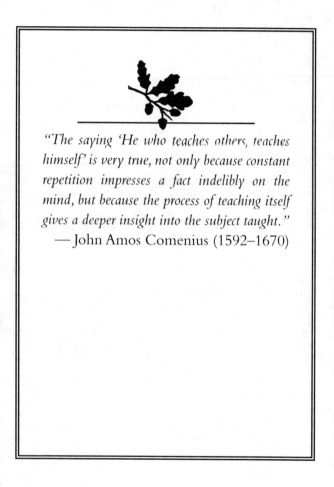

"The saying 'He who teaches others, teaches himself' is very true, not only because constant repetition impresses a fact indelibly on the mind, but because the process of teaching itself gives a deeper insight into the subject taught."
— John Amos Comenius (1592–1670)

*Seek and ye shall find; find and ye shall
want to seek a whole lot more.*

Students who learn the true excitement
and satisfaction of intellectual inquiry
will spend the rest of their days in the
pursuit of discovery.

Master persistence and then be the master.

One of the great satisfactions in life comes from accomplishing something that was thought to be impossible. This usually happens when accompanied by perseverance. If you have not learned this yet, learn it. If you have learned this, teach it.

The greatest trees are humble enough to bend in the wind.

To maintain control, you must possess enough humility to accept suffering as part of life. Avoiding suffering is like resisting the wind.

An automobile needs a driver; a classroom community needs a motivator.

Children have a positive response to the classroom environment if they are motivated. When teachers turn the key of motivation, they will get much more mileage from the class.

Complaining about your problems takes up much more time than solving them.

Everyone has problems. Those who spend their efforts solving them attract more help than those who spend their time looking for help.

It is a true leader that acknowledges all the sources of success.

When students see that a teacher draws different strengths from different sources, they are more inclined to imitate this way of life, for this is one of the secrets of success.

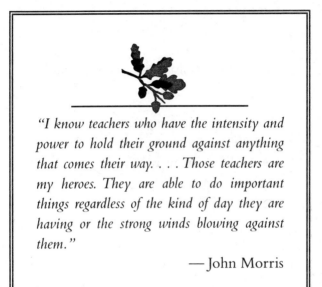

"I know teachers who have the intensity and power to hold their ground against anything that comes their way. . . . Those teachers are my heroes. They are able to do important things regardless of the kind of day they are having or the strong winds blowing against them."

— John Morris

If it excites and pleases you, show the class.

The best way to re create the excitement of discovering something wonderful is to share it. Excitement is contagious.

Compare your intentions to your habits.

When your habits reflect your intentions, the world will see you as you see yourself.

"It's important that we teach our children about each other's and other people's customs and values. We are unlikely to survive if we don't. But this does not mean that they need not hold other people's practices — and our own — up to moral scrutiny. If we do this, we confuse objectivity with neutrality."

— Albert Shanker, President,
American Federation of Teachers

There is no such thing as luck, only opportunity.

While it seems that some "have all the luck," in fact we are endlessly presented with opportunities, great and small. It is recognizing these opportunities and taking full advantage of them that creates the illusion of luck. Ignoring opportunities creates the illusion of bad luck. It is the difficult child that inspires creative teaching.

The most important victories are personal victories.

You must consistently win battles with yourself before you consistently win battles with anyone else.

No matter how often you use the same brushes and paints, each canvas will be different.

No two students are exactly alike. Develop expertise from the repetitive experiences and generate excitement from the new.

*The difference between memorizing and
learning is understanding.*

Memorizing produces familiarity, but it
is the relevant application of the lesson
that forms understanding.

Few things demonstrate the cyclical nature of life more clearly than the renewal of spring.

Spring is the eternal symbol of hope and confirmation that everything changes, and eventually, everything changes for the better.

Work is the ethic of equality.

Talent, intelligence, facility, and opportunity are all great assets. Each without hard work is wasted. Hard work alone will outshine any other asset.

It is not perfection, but the aspiration that is important.

None of us will ever achieve perfection. We also will never achieve our full potential if we don't constantly strive for perfection.

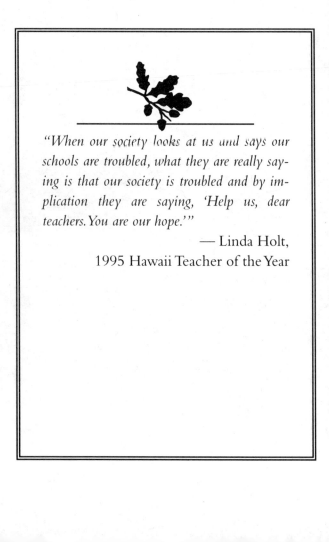

"*When our society looks at us and says our schools are troubled, what they are really saying is that our society is troubled and by implication they are saying, 'Help us, dear teachers. You are our hope.'*"

— Linda Holt,
1995 Hawaii Teacher of the Year

Decisions, not environment, rule our actions.

Behavior is controlled by us; we are not controlled by behavior.

We own nothing.

We are merely the keepers and caretakers of everything we have. We must constantly work to maintain and improve our skills, our knowledge, and ourselves to retain our rights for as long as possible.

Respect every viewpoint for what it is.

No two people can stand in the exact same place at the exact same time.

"The best homework during kindergarten is to surround kids with appropriate books and read to them 365 days a year."

— Allan S. Vann

Be who you appear to be.

When you become completely honest with yourself, integrity will eclipse any semblance of inadequacies you fear others will perceive.

Strength is the fruit on the tree of challenge.

All the physical exercise of a lifetime will not produce the strength you will gain by meeting one difficult challenge and con-quering it.

The mind has wings.

———————

Teach a child's mind to fly and you will make the concept of mental limitations obsolete.

April

Lack of motivation is sometimes born of lack of achievement.

If nothing is ever won, it becomes difficult to continue to fight the battle. It is the satisfaction of minor advances that whets one's appetite for larger victories.

Children are most interested in those who are interested in them.

We all remember that one special teacher who influenced us in so many ways. Invariably, he or she was the one who took a special, personal interest.

To be a good leader, you must be a good manager.

The most inspirational are those most in control. Those most in control lead well-managed lives.

"Some teachers say, 'I can't compete with television or video games. I can't be expected to entertain kids.' How about engaging them, then. The name of the game is inventing new ways of engaging students' minds with real work."

— Robert W. Cole and
Phillip C. Schlechty

To see clearly, learn from a child how to open your eyes.

Learning takes place in an environment where ideas replace boundaries. Children learn more readily than adults because their views are not so constricted by preconceptions.

We are blessed with the rain as we are with the sun, with the night as with the day.

Happiness comes from within. Things "make" us happy only if we are receptive. Be prepared to enjoy life's offerings, and happiness will far outweigh sorrow.

The greatest obstacle to reality is ego.

When it is the ego that is presenting the assessment, *caveat emptor!*

"I should . . . prefer the broad daylight of a respectable school to the solitude and obscurity of a private education. For all the best teachers pride themselves on having a large number of pupils and think themselves worthy of a bigger audience."

— Quintilian (ca A.D. 35–ca. 100)

When betrayal is chosen over loyalty, it is the community that suffers.

When children have a sense of worth within the class, they will feel loyalty to the group and will perceive achievement as contribution to the community.

Understand conformity and you will be able to accept rebellion.

Rebellion is a campaign to find one's identity. For most, it is a desire to belong to a group already established but at odds with the establishment. When self-expression is respected for what it is by the establishment, the rebels will spend less time in rising up.

All human progress begins with the teachers.

Teaching is what you do, learning is what students achieve, a better world is what is accomplished.

Anger is acceptable; temper is not.

The difference between venting one's anger and losing one's temper is control. One does not lose control; it is relinquished to someone else.

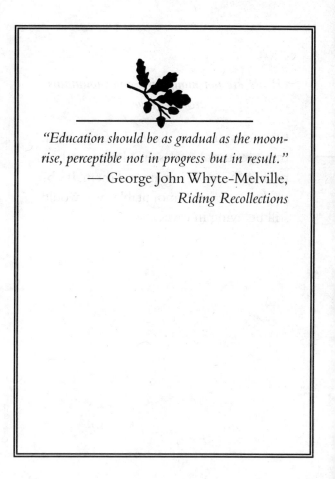

"*Education should be as gradual as the moonrise, perceptible not in progress but in result.*"
— George John Whyte-Melville,
Riding Recollections

*Walls are not mountains and mountains
are not graves.*

Obstacles are not the end of the road,
they are just obstacles. It is human nature
to find a way over or around them. If obstacles were insurmountable, we would
still be living in caves.

Do what must be done.

Often, teachers are required to operate under government mandates without government support. It is the "impossible" that leads to resourcefulness. You do not teach for your government, you teach for your students . . . and for yourself.

Even a zephyr tugs at the roots of each blade of grass.

Every breath, every word, every move ment sets unimaginable sequences in action. The power that each of us wields to change things is beyond comprehension.

You go where you look.

Focus on opportunities and travel the highway of life. Focus on problems and trudge the swamp of defeat.

Anticipate, plan, control, relax.

Panic exists in an uncontrollable environment. Uncontrollable environments are those that were not anticipated. Hope for the best, expect the worst, plan your responses in advance, and take comfort in your control.

Lure a hungry dog with food.

First, entice a student to perform with a bribe; next, get the student to perform for rewards; finally, make the performance the reward.

"Given particular subject matter or a particular concept, it is easy to ask trivial questions or to lead the child to ask trivial questions. It is also easy to ask impossibly difficult questions. The trick is to find the medium questions that can be answered and take you somewhere. This is the big job of teachers and textbooks."

— David Page

Compassion is the soul of community.

Compassion is the virtue that rewards us with another's pain. When we share pain, we share in the triumph over pain.

When you compete with yourself you have a worthy adversary.

If you attempt to show someone the error of their ways by comparing them with someone else, you will foster animosity. Show them their faults in comparison with their own strengths, and you foster a drive for excellence.

Life is struggle.

———————————

Those who seek to avoid this premise never taste the sweetness of life.

Make no judgments before tests. Assume no test is an absolute measure of accomplishment.

The phenomenon of exceeding personal limits is a daily occurrence. Judge not the accomplishment but the potential.

The success of progress is in the reduction of waste.

Each day efforts are wasted with anger, time is wasted with nonproductive efforts, and we blame our lack of accomplishment on lack of time. Waste less and you will accomplish more.

A seed is a potential flower.

Each child has the potential to bloom. The teacher is the gardener who provides the proper nutrients and the environment for the seed to reach its full potential.

All teachers teach history to those who will make history.

Everything that is taught was discovered, created, accomplished, or improved by someone before. All knowledge, then, is destined to be used and/or improved upon by those who absorb that knowledge.

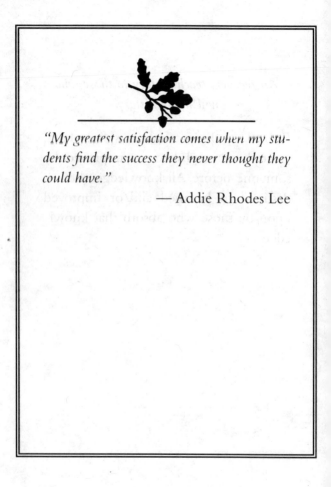

"My greatest satisfaction comes when my students find the success they never thought they could have."

— Addie Rhodes Lee

Without an audience, the song is never as sweet.

Appreciate those who appreciate you. Take another's esteem for granted, and the esteem will cease. Without appreciation the value of what we do is diminished.

The best flower won't grow in the worst dirt, but the poorest flower will thrive in the richest loam.

Those students fortunate enough to find their roots in the most nurturing teachers will always excel.

May

Intentions may be written in pencil; commitments should be carved in stone.

Everyone should *intend* to do the right thing, but *commitments* should be made only when unconditional, single-minded dedication can be employed. Much disappointment is caused by the confusion of these two words.

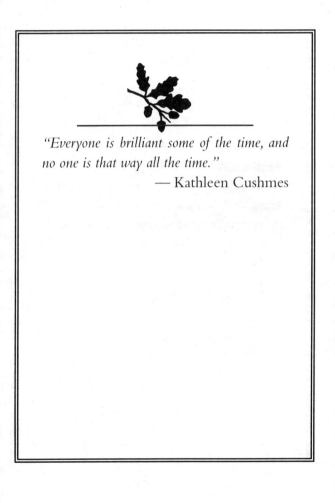

"*Everyone is brilliant some of the time, and no one is that way all the time.*"
— Kathleen Cushmes

Trust is rooted in performance.

There are many opportunities to earn trust, but there are very few second chances. Be honest at all costs, promise only that which you can do, and do everything you promise. The simplicity of this formula belies its true worth.

Confidence is the mother of incentive.

———————————

Children can accept being wrong when they know their thinking has merit. When they believe that they are just wrong, their life has little value.

Words are like golf strokes: the fewer you use, the higher they score.

In anger and in peace, choose your words. Impact is in the quality not the quantity.

The balloon of expectation should never fly farther than the string of reality.

Overinflated expectations usually result in burst aspirations.

*Motives for giving are more important
than the gift.*

To give from pity provides a meal for the moment. To give from love provides hope for life.

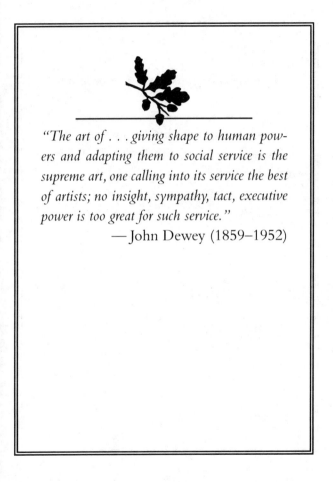

"*The art of . . . giving shape to human powers and adapting them to social service is the
supreme art, one calling into its service the best
of artists; no insight, sympathy, tact, executive
power is too great for such service.*"
— John Dewey (1859–1952)

A day of accomplishment is a good day.

To feel good about life, know the feeling of accomplishment. To know the feeling of accomplishment, accomplish something.

*The framework of a successful community
is its rules.*

Rules must be clear, fair, universal, cover all anticipated situations, and there must be a rule for situations that aren't covered. When these guidelines are understood by all, everyone knows what is expected, and self-discipline starts to form.

Possessing ambition leads to success. Being possessed by ambition leads to failure.

Ambition without priorities is wasted effort. Focusing on a destination without planning each step in between often leads to failure. When each step is taken in an individual priority, and the correction of failure becomes the basis for future success, the goal becomes the sum of the journey, and every step a learned lesson.

"When the hard times come, I think the only thing that enables me to bring the best I have to my work is a sense of vocation."

— John Morris

The pure beauty of a child's imagination is that it is unfenced by adult pragmatism.

There are fewer boundaries when one is unaware of them.

The child who is the least creative is the child who is most fearful of failure.

Trying ultimately leads to success, but success can never happen without trying. Teach children that trying is far more important than succeeding. . . . Then stand back and watch the miracle that is the human mind.

Touch a child's heart and you will be remembered. Touch a child's mind and you will be venerated.

Teachers have more opportunity to be revered than any other member of the community.

"*The trick is to create an environment that's purposely planned — and then step back and observe how the students are thinking. The planning takes a lot more time than moving from page to page in a textbook, but the reward is in the creativity.*"

— Marian Peiffer

No one can detect a counterfeit personality quicker than a child.

If you are ever to own respect, you must be genuine. Spend less effort at being someone you're not and you will have more time to be a better you.

The problem is not the problem; the problem is the solution to the problem.

A problem should be nothing more than a notification that it is time to start looking for the solution. Solutions are not found when they are not sought. Learn this well, and you will do well to teach it.

Character is paramount to natural ability.

Some are blessed with physical or mental facility, but none are more prized than the one who has developed true character.

Bad habits are hard to break but easier to replace.

Rather than attempting to "cure" yourself or someone else of a bad habit, exchange it for a rewarding practice.

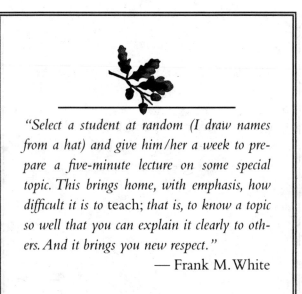

"Select a student at random (I draw names from a hat) and give him/her a week to prepare a five-minute lecture on some special topic. This brings home, with emphasis, how difficult it is to teach; that is, to know a topic so well that you can explain it clearly to others. And it brings you new respect."

— Frank M. White

To see yourself in a different light, look through someone else's eyes.

It is not necessary to accept everyone's advice, but you will understand yourself better if you listen.

He is wealthiest who gives the most.

Teachers are the most generous with their knowledge, time, wisdom, and love as part of their everyday life. The compensation for these gifts transcends the acknowledgment.

Stop only when there is nothing left to do.

You will know fulfillment in your life when you can constantly strive for perfection with the knowledge that you will never achieve it.

Rest is an enjoyable reward for hard work, but it is also necessary for continued effort.

You will perform to your full potential only when you learn how to regenerate your enthusiasm. Spend some time with yourself.

All of the lessons are only as good as the examples set by the teacher.

Students glean much more from actions than from words. You must live it to teach it successfully.

The nuances of language mirror the nuances of the senses and ultimately the nuances of life.

Looking versus seeing; listening versus hearing; breathing versus smelling; eating versus tasting; touching versus feeling: Embrace these nuances and you will begin to better understand the bitterness, as well as the sweetness, of life.

"*The true teacher defends his pupils against his own personal influence. He inspires self-distrust. He guides their eyes from himself to the spirit that quickens him. He will have no disciple.*"

— Amos Bronson Alcott,
Orphic Sayings, the Teacher

You cannot love without respecting.

If you are falling out of love with your profession or people close to you, find out why you are losing respect for them. Correct this problem and you will find love again.

Successful communities provide the environment for individuals to reach their full potential.

The nurturing family or classroom provides the "nutrients" for children to develop beyond that from which they came.

Knowledge is never a substitute for experience.

Even those who have not acquired vast stores of knowledge have something to teach from their experiences. Listen rather than judge and there is always something to learn.

June

When authority does not allow children to question everything, the children will question authority.

The answers given to children will not always be what they want, but the process of discovery is vital if they are to feel a part of the community.

Compassion and discipline are a compatible paradox.

Each alone may suggest an antithesis of the other, but when employed in conjunction they complement one another and produce real growth.

It is common to lose faith in the absence of miracles; but are you not surrounded by miracles every day?

Look not for the magic of Merlin, but witness the true miracles: a flower blooming; a child learning.

Help someone when they truly need it.
Help yourself when they don't.

When encountering another's weakness
how you react says more about you than
about the problem you perceive. Sometimes the best you can do as a person is
just to be a better person.

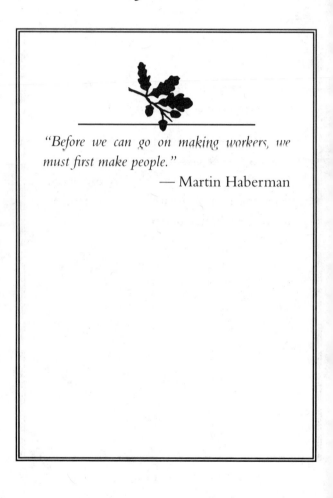

"Before we can go on making workers, we must first make people."

— Martin Haberman

For the teacher, harvesttime
Comes at the end of spring.
The seedlings of ten months ago
Are awe inspiring.
Some have grown beyond their reach,
And some have plugged along,
But each has felt the rain and sun
And heard the master's song.
Not everyone will be the fruit
That feeds the hungry world.
But each has leaves that wave as flags
Their teacher has unfurled.

"Won't it be wonderful when children learn that they can ask questions without fear?"

— Jimmie E. Cook

Strength is either gained or lost.

Strength of mind or body is never stagnant. You must regularly exercise both to increase the strength or you will certainly lose it.

If the samurai's sword is drawn, it must taste blood.

The Japanese samurai is bound by a code of honor to commitment. The sword is never used as a threat. If he draws his sword against someone and then for any reason cannot follow through, he must use the sword to take his own life. This consequence ensures that commitments are never made lightly, and so there is never any doubt about the sincerity of a commitment. The person capable of commitment to a cause is entitled to the highest trust and respect.

*Give of love freely and you will be paid
with great joy.*

As the story of your life is written, you
will find the happiest chapters were the
ones in which you shared love.

The right decision is the correct decision.

———————————

Decisions can be made with the heart or the mind but should never be made with the ego.

Experience enables us to make better, faster decisions only if we have learned from that experience.

Rather than dwell on bad choices in the past, study what went wrong and prepare for better choices in the future.

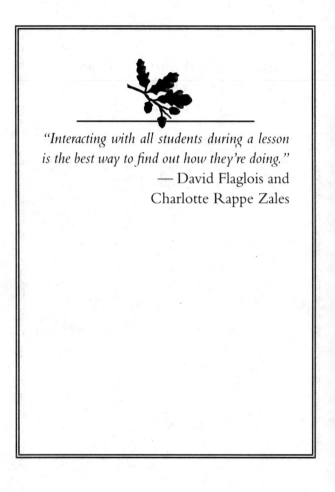

"*Interacting with all students during a lesson is the best way to find out how they're doing.*"
— David Flaglois and
Charlotte Rappe Zales

Everything has a purpose.

Even the cataclysmic destruction of a forest fire clears the path for rebirth. Seek the promise of the future in the lessons of the past.

Never substitute for integrity.

Live by your convictions and others will seek your approval. Seek approval for your actions and you'll lose your self-respect.

Humiliation is the cleanser that removes the ego to reveal the fool.

There is a price to be paid when a sense of the true self is forgotten. Honesty is much less expensive than humiliation, but humility learned is honesty bought.

"Perhaps teachers must be good actors where lessons are concerned, but in life outside the class, we mustn't hide from our pupils our individual spirits."

— Larisa Kuznetssova

Enjoy the fantasy; don't chase it.

When fantasies are a rest stop, the journey is a pleasure. When fantasies are the destination, the journey will end in a collision with reality.

An hour on a lake is a day in the city.

The measurement of time is mathematical. The *perception* of time is relative. We cannot change the mathematics, but the duration of time can be increased. We "can't find the time" because we are looking in the wrong place.

The result of winning a conflict may be perpetual contests.

Winning is only winning when it is absolute. Sometimes compromise is a greater victory than victory is.

The denser the mass, the greater the force of gravity.

Inject more meaning into fewer words and they will carry more weight.

Timing is as important as ability.

If your progress has hit a roadblock that you can't get around, it may not be your ability but your timing that is off. Back up, wait for the roadwork ahead to be completed, and try again.

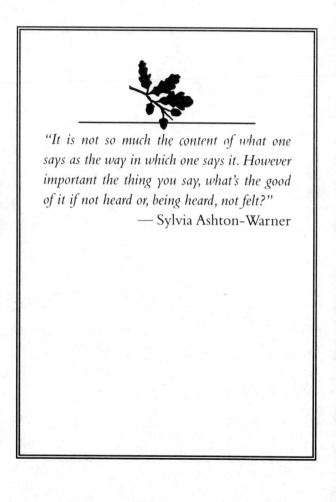

"It is not so much the content of what one says as the way in which one says it. However important the thing you say, what's the good of it if not heard or, being heard, not felt?"

— Sylvia Ashton-Warner

*Even the greatest mountain climbers
use a guide.*

When confronting life's upheavals it is wise to reach out. Faith, family, or friends may see clearly what is out of focus to you.

The seed can only propagate if it is planted.

The most secure people offer to share the knowledge of their success and their successes multiply. The insecure will take their secrets to the grave intact.

Look not at, but in.

We are each burdened with prejudice: against the poor or the rich, the smart or the slow, the gaunt or the obese. It is natural to develop prejudices. It is noble to rise above them.

Before you begin to repair it, make sure it's damaged.

When things aren't going right, it's natural to look for something to fix. Ask yourself first: Is it broken or is it just wrong?

"*A caring teacher hands children their passport to the future.*"

— Jenlane Gee

Prime the pump.

It may sometimes be necessary to create a situation in which a child can succeed for the sole purpose of honoring the achievement. Once the flow has begun, the allure of success becomes the force of gravity.

To be well rounded, one must know both sides of the circle.

Children who have never known success must be taught how to succeed. Children who have never known failure must be taught to accept failure.

July

Societal growth takes place when your viewpoint exceeds your own private world.

You must become aware of and involved in the community if you are to contribute to its growth. To live in the community without taking part is to relinquish a say in its direction.

As everything around you changes,
so must you.

Reevaluation and self-examination should take place when you can spend time in your own company. Decide where you are going and, based on experience, determine the best way to get there.

The deeper you travel into yourself, the closer you will be to the state of grace.

There is a state in which all things are in balance and insight is clearer than it's ever been. This is the state of grace. Seek it, for it is rare and perfect.

*Independence is achieved through
interdependent cooperation.*

We are all free because of the group efforts of like-minded people who have
worked and fought together to provide
freedom and keep it. Freedom is never
free.

Before you act, ask: "What do I know?"

Maturity is reached when experience becomes the basis for decision. If you do not take your experiences into consideration before you act, you cannot claim maturity.

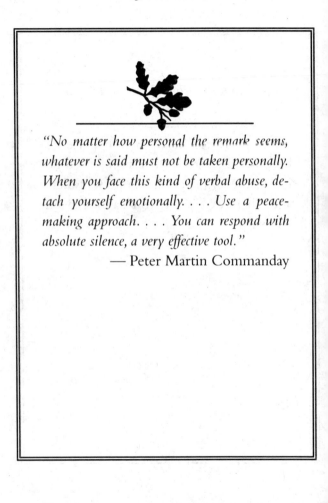

"No matter how personal the remark seems, whatever is said must not be taken personally. When you face this kind of verbal abuse, detach yourself emotionally. . . . Use a peacemaking approach. . . . You can respond with absolute silence, a very effective tool."

— Peter Martin Commanday

Be yourself lest you become those before you.

Work daily on developing your individual nature and you will know freedom. Do not, and you become the person everyone else says you are.

If you can't hear your heart, listen to your own voice.

Sometimes the act of opening up to someone frees the shackled voice and you open up to yourself.

Sit in judgment only of yourself.

Each judgment you make will be accurate or dishonest. If you are honest, you are ultimately the best judge of yourself.

Do the work!

If you are to prevail over one bad trait, choose laziness. After that, you can accomplish all things.

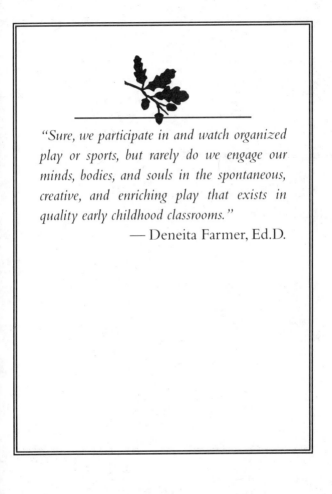

"Sure, we participate in and watch organized play or sports, but rarely do we engage our minds, bodies, and souls in the spontaneous, creative, and enriching play that exists in quality early childhood classrooms."

— Deneita Farmer, Ed.D.

*Most of what we don't know about
ourselves is in our subconscious.*

Many live their lives taking the wrong paths and make the wrong decisions primarily because they avoid doing the hard work of self-examination. The result, of course, is harder work.

Those who have it all never stop seeking.
Those who stop seeking never have it all.

The most learned profess to be but students, the most athletic are still working on their form, and those most at peace will tell of their daily inner struggles. It is not false modesty; it is fact.

Plan your day, live your plan.

———————————

One of the key ingredients in developing self-discipline is structure. This is a clear truth for adults and an absolute truth for children.

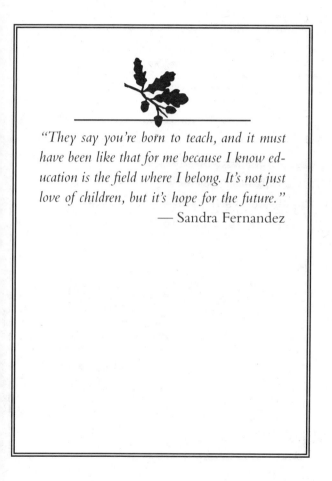

"They say you're born to teach, and it must have been like that for me because I know education is the field where I belong. It's not just love of children, but it's hope for the future."
— Sandra Fernandez

Everything in life is cyclical.

This axiom provides a warning; if things are going well, prepare yourself. It also provides eternal hope. No matter how bad things are, they must eventually improve.

Appreciate appreciation.

This thing called appreciation is rarely given the recognition it deserves. Of course, it feels good to be appreciated, but the sheer enjoyment of the sun on your face, the smell of the sea, and the giggle of a baby gives true meaning to the word.

Practice calm during the calm to better prepare for the storm.

The ability to be calm in a crisis is the mark of the master. It is also the single best antidote for fatigue. During the slow pace of summer, go to that calm place in your mind often. You will know few things more valuable than this technique.

Courtesy is the stepladder to respect.

One of the casualties of our modern fast-paced society is courtesy. It is vital to civilization that we don't let this simplest of honors die. Its destiny is in the hands of the children, and, therefore, the teachers.

Always be positive.

That a positive approach gets better results is widely known — and easily forgotten. Every response to every situation
can be presented in a positive manner.
The reverberations of this technique go
on forever.

*Character, ethics, and a sense of value are
the mutual funds of personal wealth.*

True wealth can never be lost or stolen. It
can only be shared with others or con-
verted into moral bankruptcy.

It is only work if you don't enjoy it.

———————————

Teaching is one of those vocations that becomes a job only when you no longer want to do it.

*The best security in life lies in your
ability to perform.*

A professor may be tenured, but it is the
talented teacher who is sought.

Without heat and pressure there would be no diamonds.

It is the tough situations that provide opportunities to sparkle.

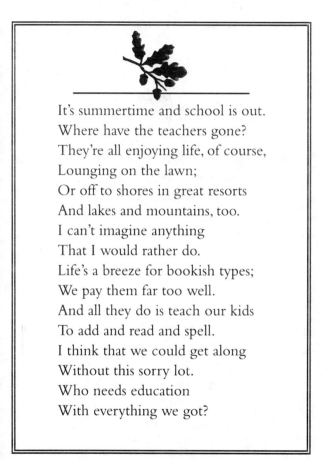

It's summertime and school is out.
Where have the teachers gone?
They're all enjoying life, of course,
Lounging on the lawn;
Or off to shores in great resorts
And lakes and mountains, too.
I can't imagine anything
That I would rather do.
Life's a breeze for bookish types;
We pay them far too well.
And all they do is teach our kids
To add and read and spell.
I think that we could get along
Without this sorry lot.
Who needs education
With everything we got?

"*It is remarkable how easily and unsensibly we fall into a particular route, and make a beaten path for ourselves.*"

— Henry David Thoreau
(1817–1862)

You can fly a kite no matter which way the wind blows.

Things rarely happen the way we would like. Be adaptable and focus on what you do, not what you get.

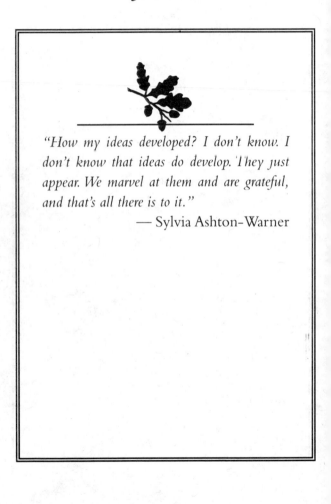

"How my ideas developed? I don't know. I don't know that ideas do develop. They just appear. We marvel at them and are grateful, and that's all there is to it."

— Sylvia Ashton-Warner

The higher you get the farther you see.

———————————

One cannot see past a mountain from its base, but once climbed it will provide the perch for new and wonderful views. Vision is at its most insightful when great obstacles have been conquered.

Drive or be driven.

A victim is someone who has either chosen to surrender control or has lost it to a
greater force. Prepare yourself to regain
control and live as you wish.

Move on.

Deal with painful decisions as quickly as you deal with pleasurable choices and find strength in balance.

August

Cherish the children; their time is fleeting.

One of the charms of childhood is that the concept of time is unlinked from that of adults. We have them for a brief moment, and they have us for their entire childhood.

There are teachers and then there is everyone else.

Anyone can read a text to a class, but a teacher teaches. Presenting new information to students in a form that they may learn it is the purview of the master. Anything less is less.

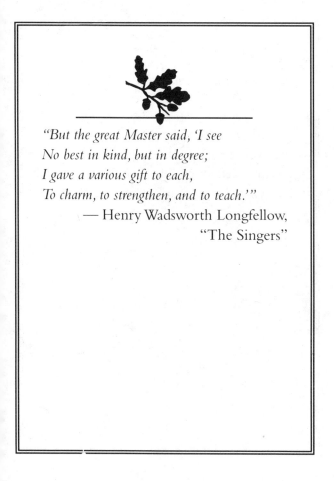

"*But the great Master said, 'I see*
No best in kind, but in degree;
I gave a various gift to each,
To charm, to strengthen, and to teach.'"
 — Henry Wadsworth Longfellow,
 "The Singers"

Self-control is a function of self-discipline.

So many weaknesses took root as bad habits that we, as children, didn't want to control. Self-discipline, like language, is best taught at the earliest possible age.

Close out the noise if you can't hear the music.

_____

When the music of life becomes the cacophony of a city street, seek the quiet place in your subconscious. Your ears are telling you your conscious mind is full.

Be strong and you can bend. Be rigid and you will break.

Being rigid in all circumstances is like nature not changing with the seasons. Stay true to your ethics and flexible with your responses.

The nature of gravity dictates that it is impossible for the bumblebee to fly. The nature of the bumblebee dictates that it will.

People exceed their capabilities all the time when they're not aware that what they're doing is "impossible." If it were really human nature to believe something is impossible, no child would ever "fly."

*Teachers are the wagonmasters for the
pioneers of the future.*

All the knowledge — in all the books, in
all the languages, in all of history —
makes up the very beginning of what is
yet to be discovered and learned.

Taste the joy of anonymity.

___

To bring joy to someone, give. To bring joy to yourself, give anonymously.

There is no honest job without merit.
Your students will fill every role.
For every edifice erected,
There is someone who must dig the hole.

Nothing is more exciting than the prospect of something new.

The poorest people are those who have everything, for they have nothing to look forward to.

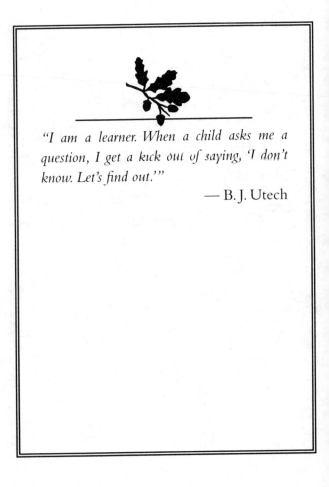

"I am a learner. When a child asks me a question, I get a kick out of saying, 'I don't know. Let's find out.'"

— B. J. Utech

Invest in children.

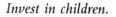

A child's life will be rich only if there are more deposits than withdrawals.

Forgive and move on.

Carrying a grudge is like filling your sack with mud: It slows you down and is without value. Forgiving is the act of dumping the mud and filling your sack with peace. It is much lighter, and you can get on with life.

The teacher becomes the subject.

When students study history, math, language, science, or any other subject, they are really studying the teacher.

It is acceptable to change fashions. It is unacceptable to change ethics.

In our ever-changing world, it is more important than ever to be morally as a rock.

Look to the head of the class; it is you!

In a world of so few positive role models, teachers have very fertile soil upon which to cast their seeds.

Be the goal your students aspire to.

Set your standards high and never lower them. Your students will understand they will be expected to come up to your example.

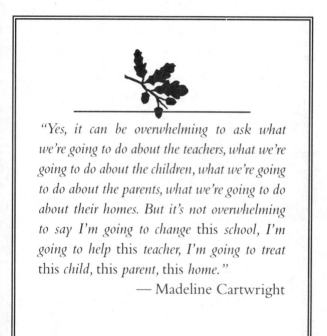

"Yes, it can be overwhelming to ask what we're going to do about the teachers, what we're going to do about the children, what we're going to do about the parents, what we're going to do about their homes. But it's not overwhelming to say I'm going to change this school, I'm going to help this teacher, I'm going to treat this child, this parent, this home."

— Madeline Cartwright

Kindness is the one gift that all can afford and all can repay.

You will never have a completely bad day if you show kindness at least once.

You'll never hear if you don't listen.

When you have taught the same class many times you will begin to believe you know every child's reaction. Every once in a while, stop and really listen. You may discover you have growing yet to do.

The teacher teaches. The master is devoted to teaching.

Prepare your lessons and you will be prepared. Devote yourself to the task, and you and your students will be rewarded beyond your imaginations.

"Teachers are the architectural designers of nations. People must see that education is not an expense, but an investment."

— Donna Oliver,
1987 United States Teacher of the Year

Trust your instincts or you will always live in doubt.

When you start to doubt yourself or your choice of professions, remember what brought you to this point in your life. Chances are it was an instinctive attraction. Trust it.

Hermits never argue.

We don't have problems understanding ourselves. We have problems understanding our interactions with others. See yourself as another sees you and you will begin to understand their viewpoint.

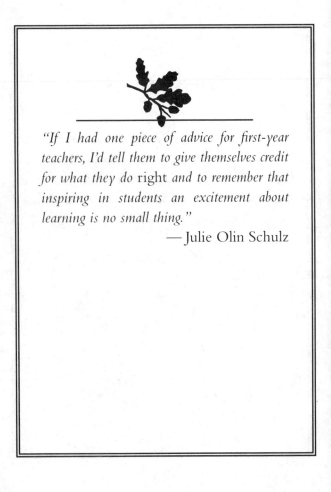

"*If I had one piece of advice for first-year teachers, I'd tell them to give themselves credit for what they do* right *and to remember that inspiring in students an excitement about learning is no small thing.*"

— Julie Olin Schulz

Everywhere you look there is a gem.

It is working with children that makes teaching the serendipitous vocation.

You cannot love without growing.

True love of oneself and of others is always accompanied by a sense of peace and spiritual growth.

The shapers of the young are the shapers of the future.

More now than ever before in the course of humankind we are on the precipice of human destiny. What happens is as much in the hands of our teachers as in anyone's.

"The kids are absolutely magnificent. It's incredible. The spontaneity, the beauty. Even though children nowadays don't have a lot of innocence in their lives anymore, they still come to us with childlike innocence, beauty, joy of life, the excitement of living. As a teacher, I get to share a little of it."

— Nancy Brice

Once again,
The master comes
To contemplate the pit,
In which sit blank
Unenlightened forms,
Each
A candle to be lit.

September

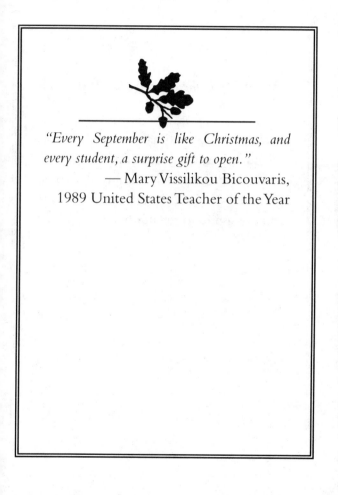

"Every September is like Christmas, and every student, a surprise gift to open."
— Mary Vissilikou Bicouvaris,
1989 United States Teacher of the Year

Personality is the clothing; character is the soul.

Each person is ultimately judged upon the quality and strength of moral convictions and principles. It is impossible to be tutored by someone of solid character and not aspire to greater heights.

Continuity and change are the comfort and fear of every child.

When a child learns to accept change without fear he or she then effects change within himself or herself by learning. A teacher should be the comfort of continuity from which new and exciting things spring.

Give children something of value and help them fight to keep it.

Some children come from backgrounds where they have little to lose. This frees them to act out because consequences have little cost. If they have something to keep (and something to lose), they will be less cavalier. Begin with dignity.

The greatest enemy in any battle is loneliness.

Few things lead to defeat more quickly than the feeling that you are fighting alone. Seek counsel with those who fight the same battle. They will often be seeking you.

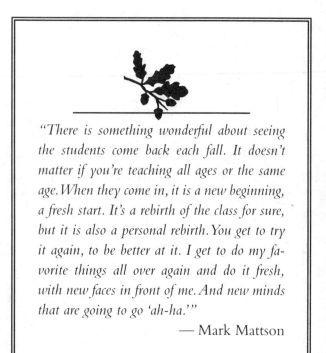

"There is something wonderful about seeing the students come back each fall. It doesn't matter if you're teaching all ages or the same age. When they come in, it is a new beginning, a fresh start. It's a rebirth of the class for sure, but it is also a personal rebirth. You get to try it again, to be better at it. I get to do my favorite things all over again and do it fresh, with new faces in front of me. And new minds that are going to go 'ah-ha.'"

— Mark Mattson

Changing your attitude is always more successful than changing your circumstances.

When your attitude is positive and determined, the task at hand is fifty percent completed. The biggest obstacle in the path to success is an attitude of self-defeat, and it is the simplest to remove.

Achievement can be accomplished only when something is attempted.

Children learn to achieve through encouragement. Some children are more adventurous than others. The formula for success must be learned. The simple act of raising one's hand to participate is a major achievement for many. When this is encouraged and then met with approval and success ("that's not correct, but it was a good try and shows you're thinking"), this achievement leads to confidence and ultimately greater achievement.

Compassion transcends ego.

Demonstrating compassion is often in conflict with "getting things done" in a busy world. Compassion for an individual in a class of many costs an unfair amount of time. But the reward of exchanging your own self-worth for a moment of understanding another's problems is always greater than any loss involved.

"Make a vow to set aside time in your life that's sacred — quiet time just for you. For a real eye-opener, keep a log of everything you do for two days. Then go back and pick out at least one thing that could have been done by someone else or didn't have to be done at all. Put stars by the things that you did just for yourself. I did this, and now I make sure to take a minivacation every day — just fifteen minutes to have a cup of tea, read a book, crochet, or talk about anything other than school."
— Joan Goodman

The difference between reality and myth is perception.

We are often disappointed because of our expectations. Only when you learn to see circumstances as they truly are can you become the architect of improvement.

Only when the masters are fully responsible for their actions can the students learn responsibility.

The ability to take responsibility is a true sign of strength and conviction. Blaming "the powers that be" is a true sign of weakness and lack of control. Take control, assume responsibility, and own respect.

Community is the basic lesson of the classroom.

It is in children's understanding of community that differences become a resource rather than a deterrent to social evolution. If the world is ever to know peace, it will be a result of the true appreciation of community.

A child can learn strength only from someone who is strong.

Inner strength is comprised of moral conviction, self-discipline, determination, and compassion. All children seek and cling to a source of strength in their lives. This strength must be present within before it can be available to those without.

The map of progress has no straight roads.

When traveling the path of progress, concentrate on the compass, not the curves.

Curiosity is the seed of knowledge.

———————————

The quest for knowledge is the result of innate curiosity in everyone. Find a way to nurture this drive in children, and they will consume knowledge as a thirsty person drinks water.

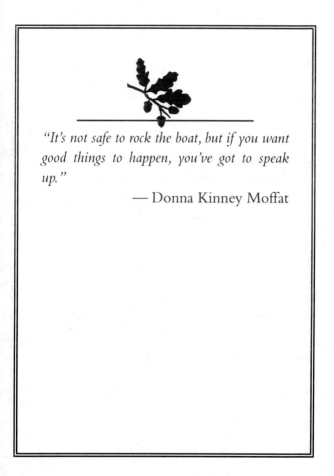

"It's not safe to rock the boat, but if you want good things to happen, you've got to speak up."

— Donna Kinney Moffat

Respect for others is born of self-respect.

A child with low self-esteem has no reason to respect anyone else. First, teach children of their own value. They will then understand how to respect others.

*Constant encouragement breeds ambition;
constant criticism breeds despair.*

Constructive criticism is an oxymoron.
Don't confuse correction with criticism.
Emphasizing positive alternatives rather
than mistakes shows a child where to go
instead of where not to go. The goal is
better performance.

Limits merely mark the point beyond which we have not yet gone.

It is not compulsory that we go beyond where we have been before. Neither should we assume that we can't. The question should never be how far, how high, how fast, or how much — but simply, how?

Roses have thorns.

Pain is a natural part of life. It should be expected, dealt with, and dismissed, so that you can get on with the beauty of life. The thorns on roses are never a surprise, and so, rarely a problem.

"I just like to help them make their dreams come true."

— Veleeta Wooten

Become what you teach.

If you are not what you require of your students, today is a great day to begin the change.

Imagination is the embryo of the future.

The powers of imagination are at their peak in children. We often don't recognize this valuable resource for what it is because we have become practical. Children can learn knowledge from adults. Adults can learn imagination from children.

Humility is the greatest expression of confidence.

When the goal of accomplishment is self-satisfaction, there is no need for fanfare. It is through silence that the message of competence is loudest.

"There will never be a single solution that will be a perfect fit for our diverse society. Don't wish for a unilateral answer to our educational dilemmas. Instead, we should work toward partnerships of families, communities, and educators who will enjoy the process of problem-solving."

— Elaine Griffin,
1995 United States Teacher of the Year

First and always, balance.

———————————

Our lives are most unmanageable when they are out of balance. When you are balanced, the difficult becomes easier and the impossible merely difficult. As you master balance, others will seek to learn from you this most obvious of secrets.

The best way to learn is to teach.

We gain more knowledge about a subject
and how to teach it from our pupils than
from any book.

Children measure their own worth by the time invested in them.

Children's perception of the quantity of time spent with them is much more acute than their perception of the quality. Listening is, in and of itself, a form of teaching, for a child learns from this act self-worth.

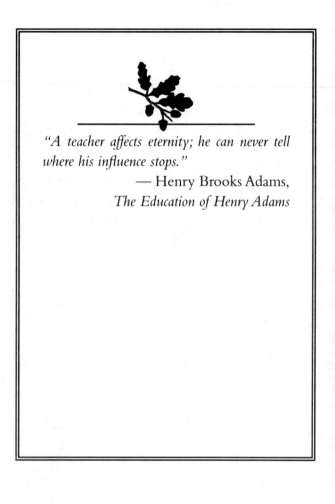

"*A teacher affects eternity; he can never tell where his influence stops.*"

— Henry Brooks Adams,
The Education of Henry Adams

October

*Sometimes the greatest way to show love
is to show no love at all.*

To love is to give of oneself, and sometimes to withhold. When one is used to
"getting," earning becomes a foreign and
avoided concept. If you can teach the joy
of earning, you have taught the blind to
see.

The more one learns, the more one sees how much is yet unlearned.

When the quest for knowledge ceases, the mind and spirit die. This is one of the most important lessons to learn and to teach.

When we give of ourselves, we gain the most.

A sacrifice made for the betterment of someone else is a gift that, by its definition, is seldom acknowledged. But through these silent acts of love, we experience our greatest growth.

Teach what you know; know what you teach.

To teach is art. To teach what you know and love is inspired. Find passion in the lesson and your teaching will be as enticing to children as sugar.

Excellence is the bull's eye.

By focusing on excellence within a goal, you will sometimes achieve excellence and almost always hit the goal. By focusing only on the goal, you will often miss the whole target.

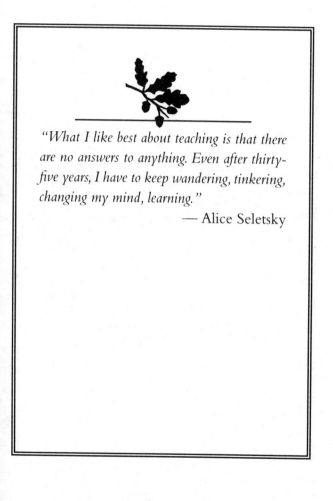

"*What I like best about teaching is that there are no answers to anything. Even after thirty-five years, I have to keep wandering, tinkering, changing my mind, learning.*"

— Alice Seletsky

Control is to stress as water is to fire.

Control will certainly alleviate stress, but, more importantly, it will *eliminate* stress. Begin each day with a plan, expect the unexpected, and it will appear that you are in control — for you will be.

Denial is a problem's nourishment.
Confrontation is its demise.

It is tempting to avoid a problem that may have an unpleasant solution, but the problem will grow with each moment of denial. Look to your heart for the answer. It is always there.

The cheapest and most valuable gift is kindness.

Kindness is not taught, it is demonstrated. Simple acts will endear loved ones forever and disarm even the most aggressive personalities.

Excitement is the bait on teaching's hook.

When a meal is presented replete with garnishes that are appetizing and interesting to the eye, the anticipation of consumption is all the greater. If you are to catch the students' interest, excite their appetites.

"No bubble is so iridescent or floats longer than that blown by the successful teacher."
— Sir William Osler, *Osler the Teacher*

Conscience is the compass; self-discipline the rudder.

In almost every situation, we know the "right" direction to take. It is natural, however, to ignore this knowledge because the right course often seems to be the most difficult. Make choices based on moral and honorable convictions, and you will be the master of your own ship.

Competition with oneself produces the strongest community.

The object of competition is the key. If you teach the pupils to compete with themselves and use their strengths to advance others, the community will grow vertically, and no one will be a stair.

Communication is the river; understanding is the ocean.

Every river leads to the ocean. The speed with which it gets there is determined by the number of dams on the way.

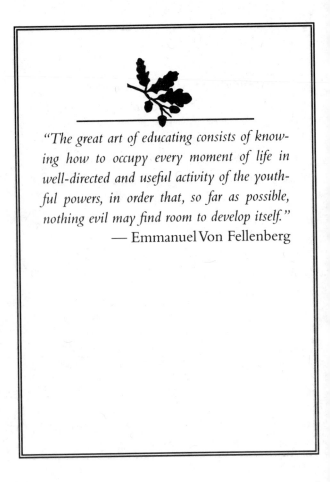

"*The great art of educating consists of knowing how to occupy every moment of life in well-directed and useful activity of the youthful powers, in order that, so far as possible, nothing evil may find room to develop itself.*"
— Emmanuel Von Fellenberg

Failure, like success, is the result of an attempt.

One cannot know the true sweetness of success without having experienced the pain of failure. It is the comparison of the two that gives each its own strength. Understand this, and you begin to understand value.

School is not a place.

All humans learn innately and a few have chosen to teach as a profession. The mere existence of the human race dictates that school will always exist without regard to, and in spite of, political, economic, and architectural parameters.

Beauty is perceived, not seen.

Beauty can be found in art, music, nature, a person's face or soul, and anything else that gives one pleasure. Everything has beauty to someone, and everyone seeks beauty. Teach your senses to perceive the beauty in all things; then teach others.

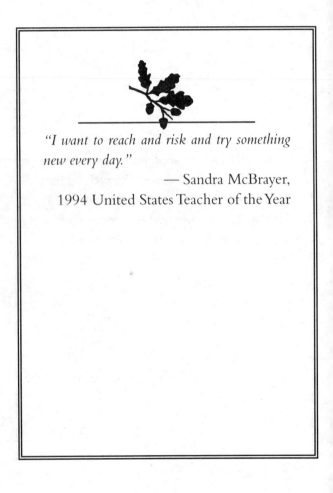

"I want to reach and risk and try something new every day."

— Sandra McBrayer,
1994 United States Teacher of the Year

Elicit commitment and respect, and you will own obedience.

It is human nature to rebel against that which we do not respect. If the teacher makes learning its own reward and respect for the master a source of comfort and guidance, obedience will be the currency for these pleasures.

Recognition easily given is recognition easily lost.

Society is willing, even eager, to worship the diverse performers that entertain us. This euphoria is easily forgotten. It is the two or three people who have taught us truth that live in our hearts and memories forever.

Strike a match in a dark room and you will understand teaching. Light a lamp with that match and you will understand knowledge.

It is human nature to seek the light. Find a way to present knowledge as the antidote for the darkness.

Quench the fires of anger and weakness with the waters of peace and strength.

In each of us there exists a lake, where peace lives and strength is born. Begin each day with a drink from its waters and go there often to refill your cup. The lake is never dry, but the path to it is sometimes hidden. The music of water, the beauty of a flower, or the depth of prayer will show you the way.

A mother gives birth to the child; a teacher gives birth to the mind.

In each case, the delivery process is equally difficult and rewarding.

The basis for a relationship is communication. The basis for a successful relationship is understanding.

Successful teaching, like a successful partnership, can only happen in an environment where everyone understands and is understood.

Many have positions of authority. Few have authority.

Children seek an authority figure to guide them. It is natural and right for them to test the validity of authority, for this is how they decide who to follow. Those without true authority rebuke these challenges. The more you anticipate and have ready your responses to challenges, the less your authority will be questioned.

The most successful government has the fewest police.

Order in the classroom, or in any community, ultimately depends on self-discipline. Teach self-discipline as an outgrowth of self-respect and self-respect as an outgrowth of self-worth, and the result will be self-improvement rather than anarchy.

To avoid being overdrawn, balance your accounts daily.

With each day our lives change. Daily self-examination provides for assessment of each success and failure. Take a moment at the end of each day to review your deposits and withdrawals. Scrutinize successes equally with failures.

Guarantees are for toasters.

Life never comes with guarantees. If you prepare yourself for success, your future will be in the hands of others. If you prepare yourself for challenges, success will be yours.

*"Let such teach others who themselves excel,
And censure freely who have written well."*
— Alexander Pope,
"An Essay on Criticism"

Fear is a primordial tool to be used, not avoided.

True fear is the conscious connection to our innate instincts, the warning signal for danger. It should be welcomed as a way to prepare for problems in advance. It is when we fail to use it as a tool that it owns us.

November

You're smart when you know the answer.
You're wise when you know you do not.

Respect is given to those who have "the answers." It is, however, quickly and almost always irrevocably withdrawn if an answer is not "the answer." One confession "I truly don't know, but I'll try to find out" is worth a million wrong guesses.

"When you work for a corporation, you get financial rewards, but you never see the results of all your hard work. With teaching, you see the results every day and the rewards are immediate."

— Margaret Coppe

Educators have a duty to teach the curricula and an opportunity to teach character.

As a student learns the subject matter from a teacher, it is inevitable that he or she learns many other things at the same time. Often, who you are is what you teach. A teacher who demonstrates character teaches character. A student who learns this, learns.

Each step should be a lesson.

For the wise person, there are only two types of experiences on life's road: winning and learning. You lose ground if you have not, in some way, advanced with each step. Find each lesson and take comfort in the knowledge you are a winner.

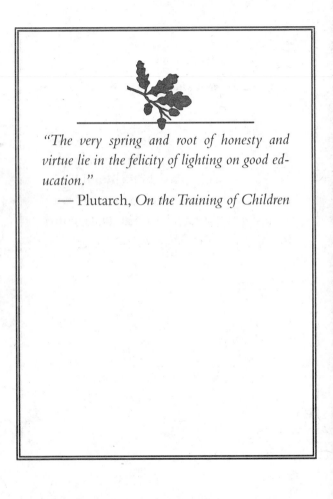

"The very spring and root of honesty and virtue lie in the felicity of lighting on good education."

— Plutarch, *On the Training of Children*

Mourn not your mistakes; mourn, rather, the missed opportunities to correct them.

Each mistake is accompanied by opportunities to correct it. These opportunities are few and fleeting. Seize them at once and know the buoyancy of peace. Miss them and live under the weight of regret.

The key to a victim's shackles is choice.

We are presented with many choices every day. They are seldom clear and painless choices, but they are choices nonetheless. When we refuse to choose, our destiny belongs to another.

The quickest way to think of a solution is to stop thinking.

Meditation, contemplation, and prayer are the highways to our subconscious. It is an empty, peaceful place where understanding is not confused by logic.

Procrastination is the daughter of fear and the sister of rationalization.

Procrastination is not born of laziness, but of fear of success, fear of failure, fear. The subsequent paralysis takes comfort in rationalizing: "I'll have time tomorrow. I've already done too much. I'm far too tired. . . ." Deal with the cause. Fear will follow if you retreat from it and retreat if you confront it.

Assess yourself with humor, and you will be able to assess others with clarity.

View yourself through the lens of humor, and you will learn what is important by seeing what is not.

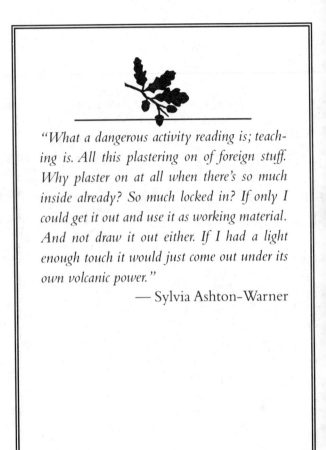

"What a dangerous activity reading is; teaching is. All this plastering on of foreign stuff. Why plaster on at all when there's so much inside already? So much locked in? If only I could get it out and use it as working material. And not draw it out either. If I had a light enough touch it would just come out under its own volcanic power."

— Sylvia Ashton–Warner

All children begin as children.

It is the rare person that can look past a social and cultural caricature and see the potential of a child. These singular individuals are often the teachers.

Consider, decide, do!

Action in the face of indecision is pure courage. It may not always turn out as expected or even hoped for, but it will be action, which is always preferable to inaction.

Study history, sculpt the future.

We are all products of past circumstances and decisions that have helped to design who we are today. Since change can only begin in the present, ignore the urge to correct the past and craft a better future.

You cannot win a battle without battling.

Shy not from the just battles. They are the proof of life and the opportunities for greatness.

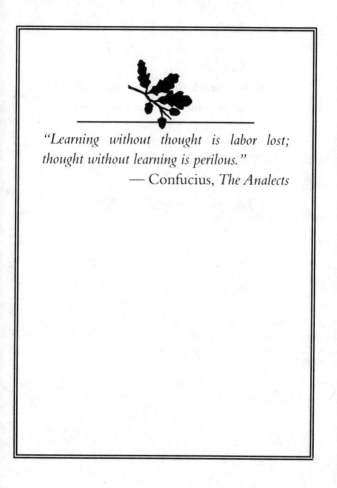

"*Learning without thought is labor lost; thought without learning is perilous.*"
— Confucius, *The Analects*

*Horizons mark the end of our sight and
the beginning of our journeys.*

It is the nature of our species to go beyond what is visible. To stimulate this
character trait in children is to foster
courage and encourage greatness.

To know freedom, live truth.

Living a life of truth is easier than most of us have come to believe. Simply endeavor to be truthful with all things. It will be more difficult at first, but with self-discipline and self-examination, it will quickly become a lifestyle rather than a goal. The permanent freedom of living with truth is greater than temporary comfort acquired in avoiding truth.

When one stops learning, one stops growing. When one stops growing, one stops.

The teacher who loves to learn is an exciting teacher.

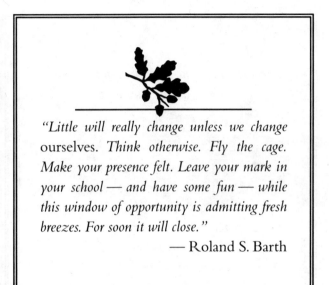

"Little will really change unless we change ourselves. Think otherwise. Fly the cage. Make your presence felt. Leave your mark in your school — and have some fun — while this window of opportunity is admitting fresh breezes. For soon it will close."

— Roland S. Barth

The first time you attempt to feed a wild animal, it will run away.

When a child that has not known much love is offered love, he or she often responds negatively and with suspicion to this unfamiliar concept. Make the offer open-ended and be prepared to spend the time to prove the sincerity of the offer. Few lessons will have greater relevance to a successful life.

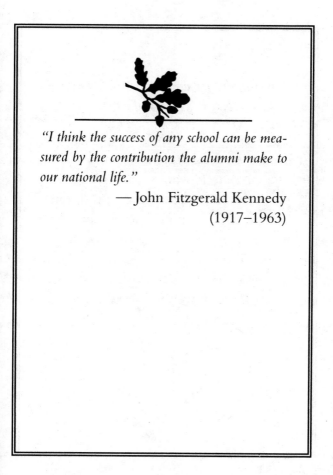

"I think the success of any school can be measured by the contribution the alumni make to our national life."

— John Fitzgerald Kennedy
(1917–1963)

Opportunity for appreciation is numbered with the grains of sand.

There are so many things to appreciate: a deed, a word, a gesture, a flower. Learning to appreciate fills one's day with endless peace and joy. Appreciating a small thing has the effect of putting everything else into proper perspective. The key is to remember to find something to appreciate in every situation. Despair is the fog through which we must search.

Values are the thread that sews the fabric of community.

The ultimate success of a society is determined by the quality of its values. The ultimate success of children is determined by the quality of education of values.

For teachers, it is better to get questions than answers.

Students who ask, show interest — the prerequisite for learning. Teach students how to ask questions in a manner that leads to the answer, and you will be teaching them the answer.

Before correcting a child's perception of the world, understand what that perception is.

We all have our own monsters. When you understand the child's, you will begin to understand yours.

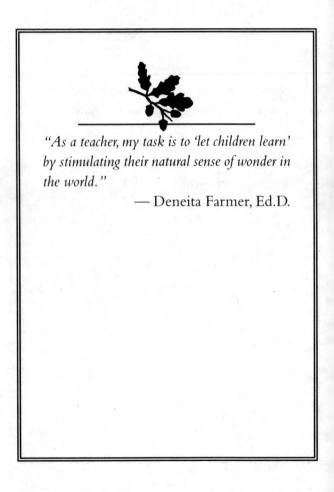

"*As a teacher, my task is to 'let children learn'
by stimulating their natural sense of wonder in
the world.*"

— Deneita Farmer, Ed.D.

It is far easier to derail a runaway train than to stop it.

Deflect anger and the aggressor will have spent his energy while you retain your balance. Attempt to stop the anger by obstructing it, and a collision must result.

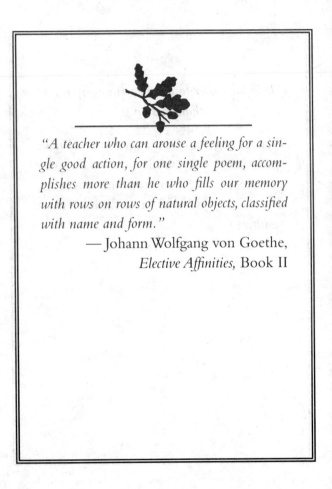

"*A teacher who can arouse a feeling for a single good action, for one single poem, accomplishes more than he who fills our memory with rows on rows of natural objects, classified with name and form.*"

— Johann Wolfgang von Goethe,
Elective Affinities, Book II

Rejoice in a child's failure, for there will never be a better opportunity to teach success.

To intuitive and encouraging hands, a failing child is soft clay. Understanding the medium is always fine art.

December

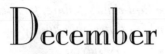

*People populate the world. Teachers
civilize it.*

The fountainhead of all the doctors, all
the artists, all the architects, all the engi-
neers, all the historians, all the scientists,
and all the teachers is the teacher.

It is the soft but continuous drip of water that will wear away and impress even the hardest rock.

The results of patience and repetition are always predictable if there is enough patience and repetition. Understand this, and you will find patience.

Take not a step, make not a move, say not a word without a clear purpose.

Objectives are often not accomplished because they are not clearly identified. Reexamine, understand, and choose *specifically* what is to be achieved each day and do only those things that will get you to this end.

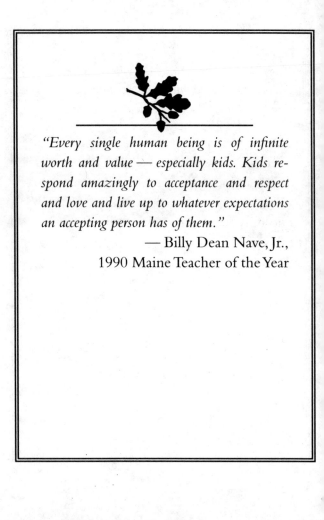

"*Every single human being is of infinite worth and value — especially kids. Kids respond amazingly to acceptance and respect and love and live up to whatever expectations an accepting person has of them.*"

— Billy Dean Nave, Jr.,
1990 Maine Teacher of the Year

The way to teach the value of life is to "live" life.

Every breath, every word, every touch is a celebration of life. When you learn how to embrace this concept, you will have transcended verbal communication, for explanations are unnecessary.

Every tree has many leaves.

Every person has weaknesses and strengths in unique combinations. To make an assessment of one's value based on a single trait would be the same as judging the condition of a tree by examining a single leaf. It takes time to view all of the leaves, and so, too, does it take time to know a person.

"If I don't get through to these children —
who knows? — maybe no one else will."
— Ivan Neal

The true difficulty for teachers is not teaching a student, but teaching a class.

Each student arrives with his or her own level of accomplishment, learning experiences, and ability. To teach beyond or behind the level of some is to lose some. The ability to tend to each individual within the context of a class is the difference between an instructor and a master.

Slay the dragon, and its remains are only those of a slain dragon.

Each problem, no matter how big, is only a part of your life and never seems as large after it has been dispatched.

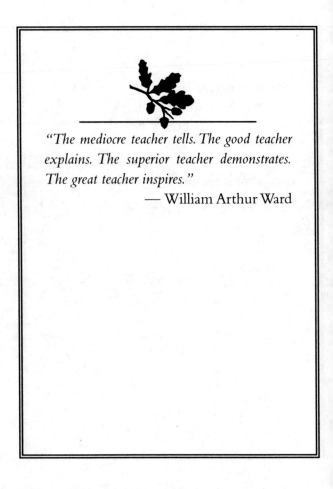

"*The mediocre teacher tells. The good teacher explains. The superior teacher demonstrates. The great teacher inspires.*"

— William Arthur Ward

Your ship can be sailed only if you are at the helm.

Taking control of your life means taking responsibility for your actions. If you refuse responsibility, you relinquish control.

To attain positive results, be positive.

There is a positive and a negative way to present every lesson in life. Excitement and encouragement are generated with the positive approach. Apprehension and discouragement are generated with the negative approach.

Success is not defined by obtaining everything you want, but by appreciating everything you have.

If the conscious mind is always occupied with getting more, it's impossible for the subconscious mind to truly savor what you've already attained. It is, then, in this constant quest for more that you ultimately lose.

Priorities are the traffic signals on the road of life.

When you ignore priorities, you are inevitably forced to run red lights and must constantly speed to catch up. The results of such a lifestyle are accidental and accidents are the result.

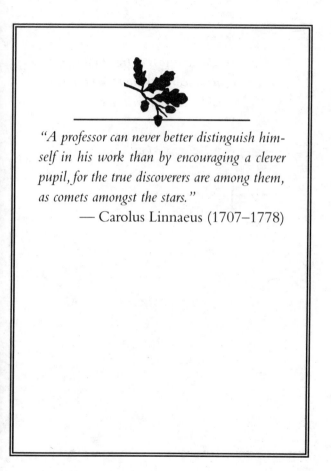

"*A professor can never better distinguish him-self in his work than by encouraging a clever pupil, for the true discoverers are among them, as comets amongst the stars.*"

— Carolus Linnaeus (1707–1778)

When you come across a tree that you do not recognize, learn its name before you consider chopping it down.

The reward for a hasty judgment is the *feeling* of superiority. The reward for the study and acceptance of what is not understood *is* superiority.

*In a changing world, only the adaptable
stay ahead.*

Everything is in a constant state of flux.
Make adaptability one of your constants
and welcome the new.

The character of a community is determined by each of its members.

The best team players are those who have the skill to act independently, the strength to assist others, and the humility to put goal above glory.

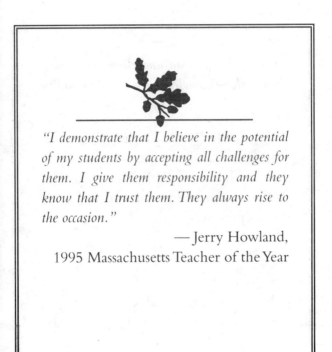

"*I demonstrate that I believe in the potential of my students by accepting all challenges for them. I give them responsibility and they know that I trust them. They always rise to the occasion.*"

— Jerry Howland,
1995 Massachusetts Teacher of the Year

Knowledge without understanding is just knowledge. Knowledge with understanding is life.

It is possible for the human mind to accumulate vast quantities of knowledge like so many stones. When understanding is the mortar, the foundation will easily support the weight of life.

It is easy to give water to the thirsty.

There are two primary environments where a child learns of his or her self-worth — home and school. If the lesson learned in school is a positive one, all subsequent lessons have greater value to the student.

Teach independence in conjunction with obedience.

When you maintain order through respect, you are teaching obedience. When you reward obedience with independence, you are teaching self-discipline.

Currency was around long before money.

The best way to get something is to give something. When students value something enough to pay the price, they begin to learn one facet of life's cause-and-effect principle.

A thing bought has little value. A thing earned is a treasure.

In this material world, acquisitions are mistaken for wealth. The true victims of this conundrum are the children.

Peace is always within reach, but sometimes out of sight.

When you feel isolated, seek out someone who is alone. When you feel forsaken, comfort one who has been abandoned. When you feel impoverished, give to the poor. When you feel unloved, love a child.

The fear of exposure often outweighs the necessity of correction.

While difficult and awkward, the experience of admitting wrongdoing clears the forest of deceit, paves the road of character, and opens up the wilderness to progress.

The potential of a child's mind is decreased by the boundaries of perceived reality.

Education is necessary for the growth of the mind. In the process of learning, however, we often confuse the ability to perceive what could be with the reality of what is. Knowledge must be the threshold of creation if there is to be progress.

The lack of confidence to excel often leads to the acceptance of merely passing.

It is better to be the best, but many have accepted that the best they can hope for is to be a little better.

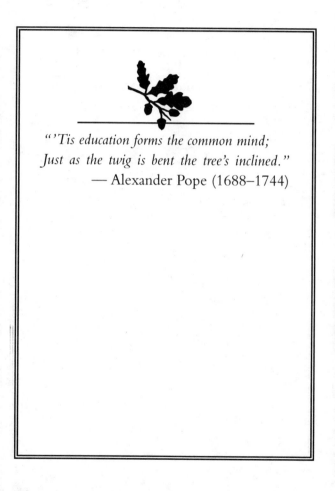

"'Tis education forms the common mind;
Just as the twig is bent the tree's inclined."
— Alexander Pope (1688–1744)

Success is only the completion of another step.

Many are disappointed when they reach their "success," and find themselves wanting for something more. Life is not a plateau to be reached, but a river to be sailed.

Each end is preceded and followed by a beginning.

Life is divided into increments: days, seasons, years, milestones, etc. That moment following the end and preceding the beginning of each of these is another opportunity to start over. This is the birthplace of eternal hope.

• BIBLIOGRAPHY •

Ashton-Warner, Sylvia. Spinster. Simon and Schuster, 1959. Teacher. Simon and Schuster, 1963.

Atkins, Andrea. "10 Great Teachers and Why They Get A's." Better Homes and Gardens, November 1991.

Barnes, Edward, and Maddox, Barbara. "The Magic Art of Teaching." Life, October 1990.

Barth, Roland S. "9 Questions We Must Ask About School Restructuring." Education Digest, December 1991.

Bartlett, John. Bartlett's Familiar Quotations. Little, Brown, 15th edition, 1980.

Brown, Jim, and Kritsonis, William Allan. "13 Ways to Be Part of the Discipline Problem." Education Digest, December 1992.

Bruner, Jerome S. The Process of Education. Harvard College, 1960.

Cartwright, Madeline, and D'Orso, Michael. Lessons From a Visionary Principal. Doubleday, 1993.

Cole, Robert W., and Schlechty, Phillip C. "Teachers as Trailblazers in Restructuring." Education Digest, February 1993.

Collins, Catherine, and Frantz, Douglas. Teachers Talking Out of School. Little, Brown, 1993.

Commanday, Peter Martin. "Practical Peacemaking Techniques for Education." Education Digest, March 1993.

Cook, Jimmie. *"Unintimidated Inquiry."* Teaching K-8, *August–September 1992.*

Cookson, Jr., Peter W., and Persell, Caroline Hodges. Preparing for Power: America's Elite Boarding Schools. *Basic Books, 1985.*

Cushmes, Kathleen. *"Seminars Benefit All Students."* Education Digest, *September 1992.*

Dewey, John. Experience and Education. *Macmillan, 1938.*

Farmer, Deneita. *"Why I Keep Teaching."* Scholastic Early Childhood Today, *August–September 1993.*

Flaglois, Donald, and Zales, Charlotte Rappe. *"Anatomy of a Top Teacher."* Education Digest, *January 1991.*

Fliegel, Seymour, and Macguire, James. Miracle in East Harlem: The Fight for Choice in Public Education. *Random House, 1993.*

Haberman, Martin. *"The Pedagogy of Poverty vs. Good Teaching."* Education Digest, *September 1992.*

Instructor, *"Making Time for What Matters." January–February 1995.*

Junior Scholastic, *"Be a Teacher. Be a Hero." April 2, 1993.*

Kane, Pearl Rock, ed. The First Year of Teaching: Real World Stories from America's Teachers. *New American Library, 1991.*

Kuznetssova, Larisa. *"A Soviet Teacher Speaks Out."* Education Digest, *October 1991.*

Miller, Mary Susan. *"Teacher of the Year."* Good House-
  keeping, *May 1987, May 1988, and May
  1989.*

Morris, John. *"Vignettes from Vermont: An Elementary
  School Teacher Reflects."* Education Digest, *December 1992.*

The New York Times, *January 5, 1965.*

Newsweek, *October 17, 1988.*

Quintilian. Institutes of Oratory, *translated by H. E. But-
  ler. The Loeb Classical Library, Harvard University.*

Sacher, Emily. Shut Up and Let the Lady Teach. *Poseidon
  Press, 1991.*

Shanker, Albert. *"The Pitfalls of Multicultural Education."*
  Education Digest, *1991.*

Thoreau, Henry David. Walden. *1854.*

Tifft, Susan. Time, *November 14, 1988.*

Vann, Allan S. *"Let's not push our kindergarten children."*
  Education Digest, *September 1991.*

· INDEX ·

• NOTES •

• NOTES •

• NOTES •